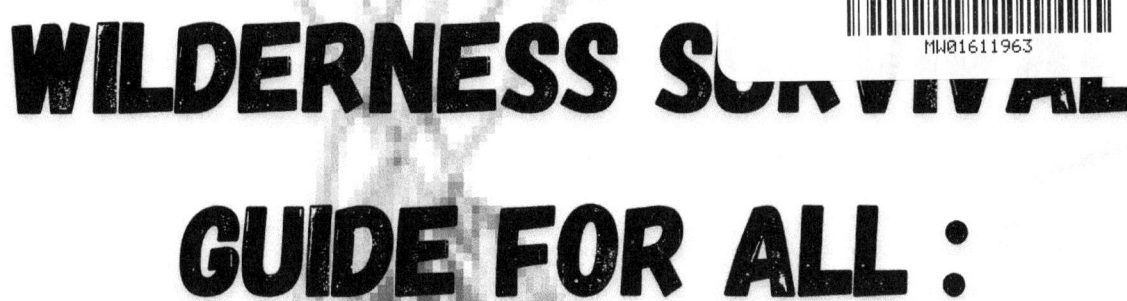

# WILDERNESS SURVIVAL

# GUIDE FOR ALL :

## A COMPLETE COMPANION TO THRIVE

## IN THE WILD.

### BY
### Bush Garrison

i

# CONTENTS

# CONTENTS

# INTRODUCTION

Embarking on a journey into the wilderness is a thrilling endeavor filled with endless possibilities for adventure and self-discovery. Whether you're a seasoned outdoor enthusiast or a novice explorer, the wilderness offers an unparalleled opportunity to connect with nature, test your limits, and uncover hidden treasures amidst rugged landscapes.

As you prepare to venture into the untamed wilderness, it's essential to approach your journey with careful planning, thoughtful consideration, and a spirit of adventure.

# INTRODUCTION

From navigating winding trails to setting up camp beneath starlit skies, each moment in the wilderness presents a chance to embrace the beauty of the natural world and forge unforgettable memories that will last a lifetime.

In this guide, we'll explore essential tips, tricks, and resources to help you navigate the wilderness with confidence, from packing the right gear to staying safe in challenging environments. So, lace up your boots, pack your backpack, and get ready to embark on an unforgettable wilderness adventure!

# GOING WITH A GUIDE BOOK

Hey there!
Don't forget to bring this guidebook along for your wild escapades! It's your trusty sidekick for navigating the untamed wilderness. From avoiding bear hugs to outsmarting sneaky squirrels, this book has got you covered! So grab your backpack and let's get wild darling.

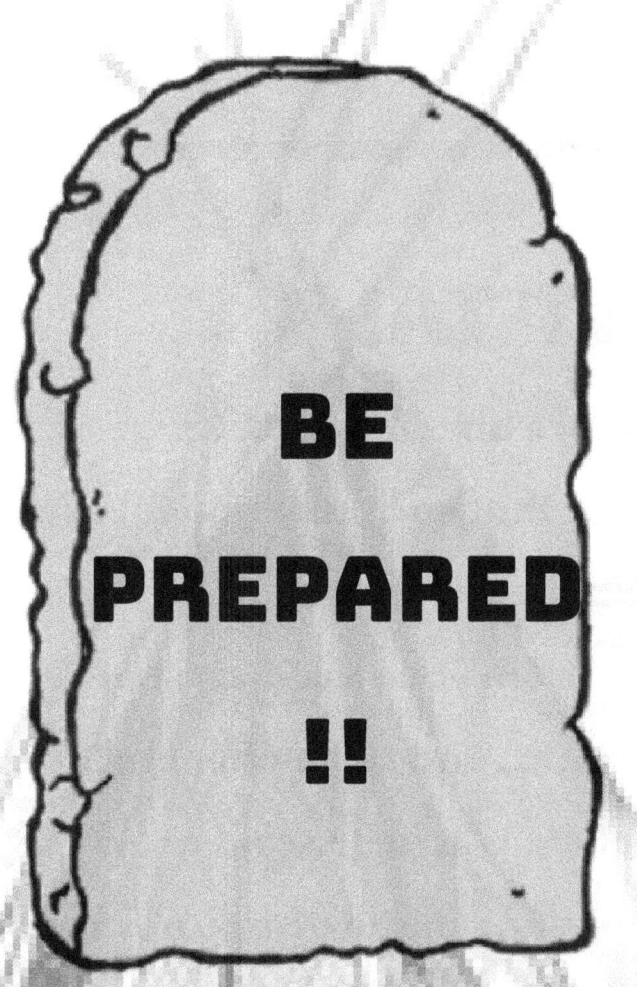

# BE
# PREPARED
# !!

Embarking on a wilderness journey with friends can be an exhilarating and rewarding experience, but it's essential to prioritize safety and preparedness to ensure a successful trip. Here are some key steps to help you stay secure and survive for a week in the wilde

# PEP TALK

Embrace the adventure ahead with courage and enthusiasm, knowing that each step you take into the wilderness holds the promise of discovery and personal growth. Trust in your abilities, stay adaptable to challenges, and remember that every obstacle is an opportunity to learn and grow stronger. Let the beauty of nature inspire you, and may your journey be filled with unforgettable experiences and meaningful moments. You've got this!

# STAYING CALM

To stay calm, focus on your breathing, taking slow, deep breaths to center yourself and ease tension. Practice mindfulness by grounding yourself in the present moment, observing your surroundings without judgment. Finally, maintain a positive mindset, reminding yourself of your capabilities and embracing challenges as opportunities for growth.

# QUICK TIP

## SAFETY PINS:

Keep a few safety pins in your survival kit for emergency repairs to clothing or gear.
Use safety pins to secure makeshift shelters or tarps in windy conditions.
It can serve as fishing hooks.

## HAIR PEGS:

Use hair pegs to keep your hair tied back and out of your face to maintain visibility while navigating trails.
Secure tarps or tents with hair pegs to provide additional stability in windy conditions.

# QUICK TIP

**DENTAL FLOSS:**

Dental floss can be used as a strong and versatile cordage for repairs or securing items in a pinch.

Use dental floss to create makeshift fishing line or snare traps for catching small game.

Dental floss can also be used to stitch minor wounds in an emergency situation.

**COTTON BALLS:**

Cotton balls are lightweight and compact, making them ideal for carrying in your first aid kit.

Use cotton balls as tinder for starting fires by coating them with petroleum jelly or other flammable materials.

Soak cotton balls in antiseptic solution to create makeshift wound dressings or use them to apply ointments or creams.

# GOING TO THE WILD AS A KID

- Always go with adult supervision or in a group with responsible adults.

- Inform a trusted adult or guardian about your plans, including where you'll be going and when you'll return.

- Stay on designated trails and paths to avoid getting lost.

- Follow safety guidelines for wildlife encounters and respect nature by leaving no trace.

<u>Permission should be obtained from a parent or guardian before venturing into the wilderness as a kid. It's important to communicate your plans with them and ensure they approve of your trip.</u>

# GOING TO THE WILD AS AN ADULT

- Plan your trip carefully, researching the area, weather conditions, and potential hazards.

- Inform a trusted friend, family member, or roommate about your plans, including your itinerary and expected return time.

- Follow Leave No Trace principles to minimize your impact on the environment and preserve wilderness areas for future generations.

# GOING TO THE WILD AS AN ADULT

- Stay aware of your surroundings, watch for signs of wildlife, and be prepared to respond to emergencies or unexpected situations.

**Permission should be obtained from a trusted friend, family member, or roommate before venturing into the wilderness as an adult. It's important to inform someone responsible about your plans and ensure they have your itinerary in case of emergencies.**

# GOING TO THE WILD AS A GROUP

- Plan the trip together, discussing the destination, route, and expectations for the journey.

- Assign roles and responsibilities within the group, such as navigation, first aid, and gear management.

- Inform a trusted individual who is not part of the group about your plans, including your itinerary and expected return time.

# GOING TO THE WILD AS A GROUP

- Stay together and communicate effectively throughout the journey, watching out for each other and making decisions as a team.

- Follow Leave No Trace principles to minimize your impact on the environment and preserve wilderness areas for future generations.

**Permission should be obtained from a trusted individual who is not part of the group before venturing into the wilderness. This person should have your itinerary and contact information and can serve as a point of contact in case of emergencies.**

# KNIFE SAFETY

**Here are some knife safety instructions to follow while in the wilderness:**

1. Before using the knife, ensure it is clean, dry, and in good condition.
2. Hold the knife securely with a firm grip, ensuring your fingers are away from the blade.
3. Always cut away from your body and keep your fingers clear of the blade's path.
4. Use slow and controlled motions when cutting or carving, avoiding sudden or jerky movements.
5. When not in use, sheath the knife or store it securely to prevent accidental cuts or injuries.
6. Never use the knife for tasks it's not designed for, such as prying or chopping hard objects.

# CHOOSING LOCATIONS

1. Research areas matching your interests and skill level.

2. Check regulations and permits required.

3. Consider terrain, weather, and accessibility.

4. Seek recommendations from experienced individuals.

5. Prioritize safety, ensuring access to emergency services and medical facilities.

6. Minimize environmental impact by following Leave No Trace principles.

16

# BASIC SURVIVAL KITS:

A SURVIVAL KIT IS A COMPACT COLLECTION OF ESSENTIAL ITEMS AND TOOLS DESIGNED TO AID YOU IN SURVIVING EMERGENCY SITUATIONS WHILE IN THE WILDERNESS:

TENT: Carry a tent in a waterproof stuff sack attached securely to your backpack .

**1**

ROPE: A rope in a survival kit is invaluable for its versatility. Make sure to go with it.

**2**

# BASIC SURVIVAL KITS:

**SNACKS:** Carry some snacks and put it in a waterproof, airtight container within easy reach in your backpack, ensuring accessibility and preservation of the snack's freshness and nutritional value.

**3**

**WARM JACKET:** Make sure to wear a warm jacket or carry one alongside with you.

**4**

18

# BASIC SURVIVAL KITS:

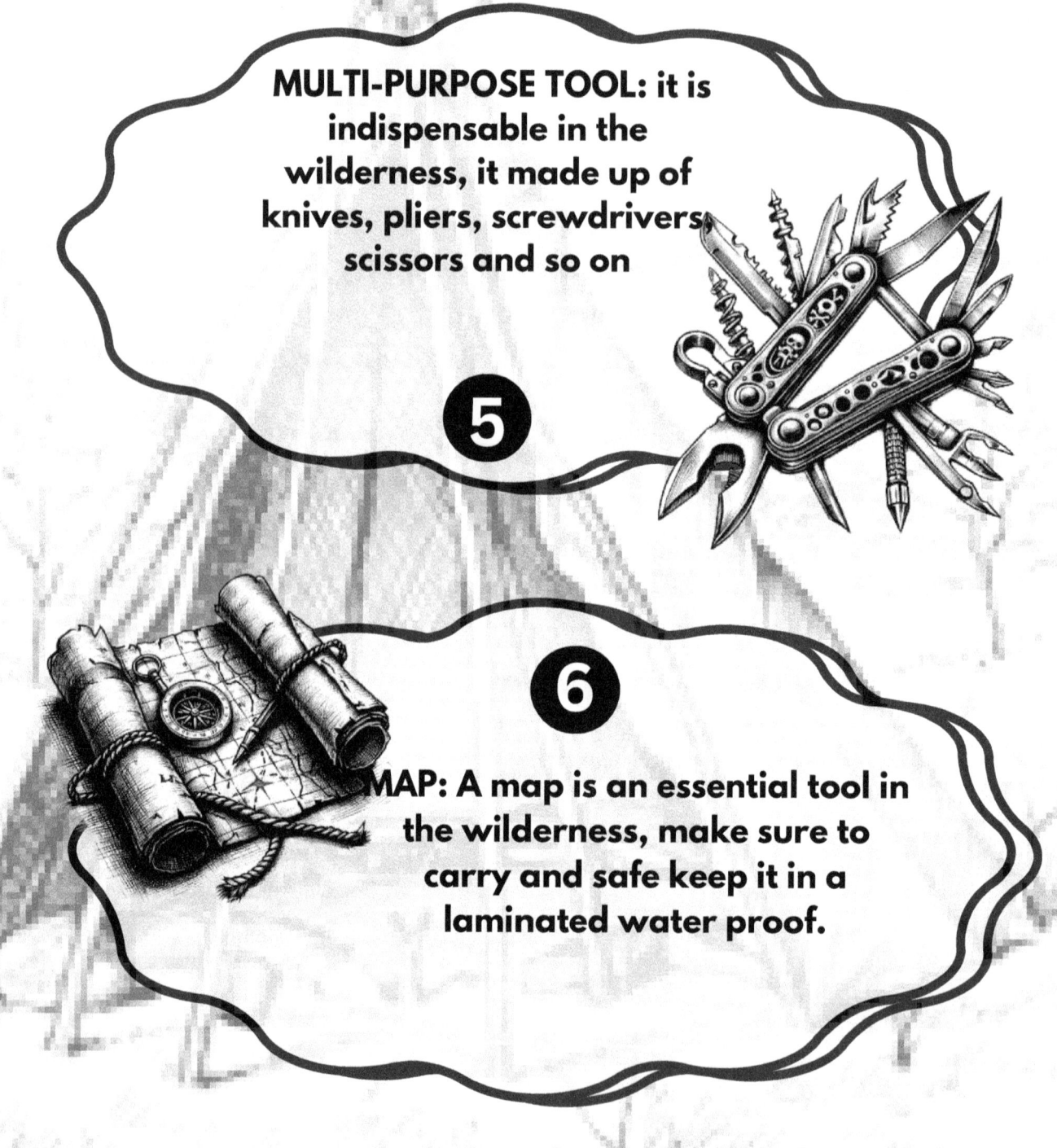

**MULTI-PURPOSE TOOL:** it is indispensable in the wilderness, it made up of knives, pliers, screwdrivers scissors and so on

**5**

**6**

**MAP:** A map is an essential tool in the wilderness, make sure to carry and safe keep it in a laminated water proof.

# BASIC SURVIVAL KITS:

**TOUCH:** Make sure to carry a touch land some spare batteries.

**7**

**8**

**WATER PURIFIER:** Very important survival kit as it will keep you healthy.

# BASIC SURVIVAL KITS:

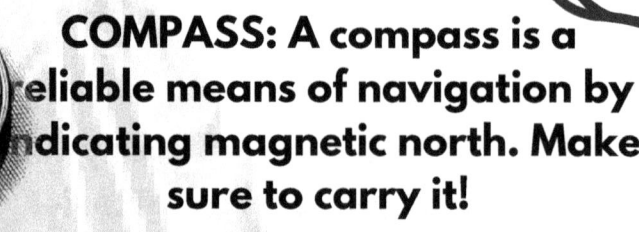

**COMPASS: A compass is a reliable means of navigation by indicating magnetic north. Make sure to carry it!**

**9**

**10**

**WATERPROOF BACK-PACK: portable storage solution for putting all the basic survival kits. You can always make preference.**

# BASIC SURVIVAL KITS:

**LIGHTER:**
A reliable means of starting fires. This is the best option compared to a match box.

**11**

**WHISTLE:** A whistle is a critical tool in the wilderness, make sure to carry one or more.

**12**

# ADDITIONAL SURVIVAL KITS:

1. Emergency radio

2. Flare gun

3. Glow sticks

4. Emergency food bars

5. Space-saving cooking set

6. Quick-dry towel

7. Hand sanitizer

8. Water-resistant notepad

9. Pen or pencil

10. Emergency shelter kit

# ADDITIONAL SURVIVAL KITS:

11. Thermal clothing

12. Insulated gloves

13. Emergency cash

14. Personal identification documents

15. Solar charger

16. Folding saw

17. Signal mirror

18. Emergency blanket

19. Firesteel

20. Paracord

21. Duct tape

22. Sunscreen

23. Insect repellent

# THE USES OF SURVIVAL KITS INCLUDE:

**1.Tent:** A tent provides shelter from the elements, offering protection against rain, wind, and insects, while also providing a comfortable and secure sleeping area in the wilderness.

**2.Rope:** Rope is essential for various tasks such as building shelters, securing gear, and creating improvised tools, providing versatility and utility in wilderness survival situations.

**3.Snacks:** Snacks provide a quick source of energy and sustenance during outdoor activities, helping to maintain energy levels and prevent hunger while exploring the wilderness.

# THE USES OF SURVIVAL KITS INCLUDE:

**4. Warm jacket:** A warm jacket offers insulation and protection against cold temperatures, ensuring comfort and warmth in chilly or inclement weather conditions while in the wilderness.

**5. Multi-purpose tool:** A multi-purpose tool combines various functions such as cutting, screwdriving, and pliers, providing versatility and convenience for performing a wide range of tasks in survival situations.

**6. Map and compass:** A map and compass are essential navigation tools for orienting oneself, determining direction, and navigating through unfamiliar terrain in the wilderness, helping to prevent getting lost.

# THE USES OF SURVIVAL KITS INCLUDE:

**7. Touch light:** A touch light provides illumination during low-light conditions or emergencies, aiding visibility for tasks such as navigating trails, setting up camp, or signalling for help in the wilderness.

**8. Water purifier:** A water purifier ensures access to safe and clean drinking water by removing harmful contaminants and pathogens from natural water sources, preventing waterborne illnesses during outdoor adventures.

**9. Waterproof backpack:** A waterproof backpack protects gear and supplies from moisture and rain, keeping them dry and secure while hiking or camping in wet conditions.

# THE USES OF SURVIVAL KITS INCLUDE:

**10. Lighter:** A lighter is a reliable and convenient fire-starting tool, enabling the ignition of fires for warmth, cooking, and signalling purposes in wilderness survival situations.

**11. Whistle:** A whistle is a lightweight and effective signalling device for attracting attention in emergencies, providing an audible alert to rescuers or fellow hikers when help is needed in the wilderness.

**12. Emergency radio:** An emergency radio allows for communication and receiving weather updates and emergency alerts in remote areas without cellular coverage, enhancing safety and situational awareness in the wilderness.

# THE USES OF SURVIVAL KITS INCLUDE:

**13. Flare gun:** A flare gun is a powerful signalling device for attracting attention over long distances in emergencies, providing a visual alert to rescuers or search parties in remote wilderness locations.

**14. Glow sticks:** Glow sticks offer low-level illumination for navigating in the dark, marking trails, or signalling for help, providing a reliable light source without the need for batteries in wilderness situations.

**15. Emergency food bars:** Emergency food bars provide compact and calorie-dense nutrition for sustaining energy and preventing hunger during extended outdoor adventures or survival situations in the wilderness.

# THE USES OF SURVIVAL KITS INCLUDE:

**16. Space-saving cooking set:** A space-saving cooking set includes lightweight and collapsible cookware for preparing meals and boiling water, offering convenience and efficiency for cooking in the wilderness.

**17. Quick-dry towel:** A quick-dry towel absorbs moisture and dries quickly, providing comfort and hygiene for bathing, drying off, or cleaning gear while camping or hiking in the wilderness.

**18. Hand sanitizer:** Hand sanitizer helps maintain hygiene and prevent the spread of germs and bacteria in the wilderness, providing a convenient way to clean hands before meals or after outdoor activities.

# THE USES OF SURVIVAL KITS INCLUDE:

**19. Water-resistant notepad:** A water-resistant notepad allows for recording notes, observations, or emergency information in wet or damp conditions, providing a reliable means of documentation in the wilderness.

**20. Pen or pencil:** A pen or pencil is essential for writing notes, marking maps, or leaving messages in the wilderness, providing a simple and versatile tool for communication and documentation.

**21. Emergency shelter kit:** An emergency shelter kit includes lightweight and compact shelters such as tarps or emergency blankets, providing protection from the elements in case of unexpected weather or emergencies in the wilderness.

# THE USES OF SURVIVAL KITS INCLUDE:

**22. Thermal clothing:** Thermal clothing offers insulation and warmth in cold weather conditions, helping to regulate body temperature and prevent hypothermia during outdoor activities or survival situations in the wilderness.

**23. Insulated gloves:** Insulated gloves provide protection and warmth for hands in cold weather conditions, ensuring comfort and dexterity while performing tasks or activities outdoors in the wilderness.

**24.Emergency cash:** Emergency cash provides a backup source of funds for purchasing supplies, transportation, or emergency services in remote areas without access to banking or ATM services.

# THE USES OF SURVIVAL KITS INCLUDE:

**25. Personal identification documents:** Personal identification documents such as IDs, passports, or emergency contact information provide essential identification and documentation in emergencies, aiding rescue efforts or medical treatment in the wilderness.

**26.Solar charger:** A solar charger allows for recharging electronic devices such as phones, GPS units, or cameras using solar power, providing a renewable energy source for staying connected and powered up in the wilderness.

# THE USES OF SURVIVAL KITS INCLUDE:

27.Folding saw: A folding saw is a lightweight and portable tool for cutting wood and branches, allowing for building shelters, gathering firewood, or clearing trails in the wilderness.

28.Signal mirror: A signal mirror reflects sunlight to create a visible signal for attracting attention in emergencies, providing a non-verbal means of communication for signalling rescuers or search parties in remote areas.

29. Fire steel: Fire steel is a reliable and durable fire-starting tool that produces sparks when struck against a hard surface, enabling the ignition of fires for warmth, cooking, and signalling purposes in wilderness survival situations.

# FIRST AID BOX:

First aid tools are invaluable in the wilderness as they provide essential medical care for injuries and emergencies that may occur during outdoor adventures. Common first aid tools include bandages, adhesive tape, antiseptic wipes, tweezers, scissors, and pain relievers.

# FIRST AID BOX:

## What you need to know

Before embarking on a wilderness trip, ensure you are familiar with how to use each first aid tool_properly and have received basic first aid training. Carry a well-stocked first aid kit and know where it is located in your pack for quick access in case of emergencies. Regularly check and replenish your first aid supplies to ensure they are up to date and ready for use.

# FIRST AID BOX:

## Common First Aid Tools and their usefulness

1. **Bandages and Adhesive Tape:** Use bandages to cover wounds and control bleeding. Adhesive tape can be used to secure bandages and dressings in place.

2. **Antiseptic Wipes:** Clean wounds with antiseptic wipes to prevent infection before applying bandages or dressings.

3. **Tweezers:** Use tweezers to remove splinters, thorns, or debris from wounds. Disinfect tweezers with antiseptic wipes before and after use.

4. **Scissors:** Use scissors to cut bandages, dressings, or clothing if needed for first aid treatment. Be cautious when using scissors near the skin to avoid further injury.

# FIRST AID BOX:

## Common First Aid Tools and their usefulness

5. Pain reliever: Administer pain relievers as necessary for pain management, following the recommended dosage instructions.

6. Emergency Blanket: Use an emergency blanket to provide warmth and protection from the elements in case of hypothermia or shock.

7. CPR Mask:  If trained in CPR, use a CPR mask to provide rescue breaths while performing cardiopulmonary resuscitation (CPR) on someone experiencing cardiac arrest.

# FIRST AID BOX:

## Common First Aid Tools and their usefulness

**8. First Aid Manual:** Refer to a first aid manual or guidebook for instructions on how to treat specific injuries or medical emergencies.

**9. Disinfectant Solution:** Apply disinfectant solution (such as hydrogen peroxide or povidone-iodine) to clean wounds and kill bacteria, viruses, and other pathogens. Use a clean cloth or cotton swab to apply the disinfectant to the affected area.

**10. Antibiotic Ointment:** After disinfecting the wound, apply antibiotic ointment to further prevent infection and promote healing. Spread

# VARIOUS TYPES OF INJURIES THAT ONE MIGHT EXPERIENCE WHILE IN THE WILD:

## SPRAINS AND STRAINS:
Resulting from twisting or overstretching of muscles, ligaments, or tendons during hiking, climbing, or other physical activities.

# VARIOUS TYPES OF INJURIES THAT ONE MIGHT EXPERIENCE WHILE IN THE WILD:

## FRACTURES:

Bone fractures can occur due to falls, accidents, or trauma while navigating rough terrain.

# VARIOUS TYPES OF INJURIES THAT ONE MIGHT EXPERIENCE WHILE IN THE WILD:

## CUTS AND LACERATIONS:

Caused by sharp objects, rocks, branches, or tools, leading to open wounds that may require cleaning, disinfection, and bandaging.

# VARIOUS TYPES OF INJURIES THAT ONE MIGHT EXPERIENCE WHILE IN THE WILD:

## BURNS:
Exposure to campfires, cooking stoves, or hot surfaces can cause burns of varying degrees, necessitating immediate first aid and proper wound care.

## HYPOTHERMIA:
Prolonged exposure to cold temperatures, wind, and wet conditions can lead to hypothermia, a potentially life-threatening condition characterized by a drop in body temperature.

# VARIOUS TYPES OF INJURIES THAT ONE MIGHT EXPERIENCE WHILE IN THE WILD:

## HEAT EXHAUSTION AND HEATSTROKE:
Overexertion in hot and humid environments can cause heat-related illnesses such as heat exhaustion or heatstroke, leading to dehydration, dizziness, nausea, and loss of consciousness.

## TRAUMATIC INJURIES:
Falls, accidents, or encounters with sharp objects or equipment can cause traumatic injuries such as head injuries, spinal cord injuries, or internal bleeding, requiring prompt medical attention.

# VARIOUS TYPES OF INJURIES THAT ONE MIGHT EXPERIENCE WHILE IN THE WILD:

## ALLERGIC REACTIONS:

Exposure to allergens such as pollen, plants, or certain foods can trigger allergic reactions, ranging from mild discomfort to severe anaphylaxis requiring immediate medical attention.

## DEHYDRATION:

Insufficient fluid intake, especially in hot and dry conditions, can lead to dehydration, causing symptoms such as thirst, fatigue, dizziness, and decreased urine output

# VARIOUS TYPES OF INJURIES THAT ONE MIGHT EXPERIENCE WHILE IN THE WILD:

## ALTITUDE SICKNESS:

Ascending to high altitudes without proper acclimatization can result in altitude sickness, characterized by symptoms such as headache, nausea, dizziness, and shortness of breath.

# VARIOUS TYPES OF INJURIES THAT ONE MIGHT EXPERIENCE WHILE IN THE WILD:

## DROWNING:
Water-related activities such as swimming, boating, or crossing rivers pose risks of drowning, especially in fast-moving currents or deep water without proper safety precautions.

# VARIOUS TYPES OF INJURIES THAT ONE MIGHT EXPERIENCE WHILE IN THE WILD:

## ANIMAL ENCOUNTERS:
Wildlife encounters, including bites, scratches, or attacks from animals such as snakes, bears, or mountain lions, pose risks of injury and require caution and appropriate safety measures

# VARIOUS TYPES OF INJURIES THAT ONE MIGHT EXPERIENCE WHILE IN THE WILD:

**EXHAUSTION AND FATIGUE:**
Overexertion, inadequate rest, and lack of proper nutrition can lead to exhaustion and fatigue, impairing judgment, coordination, and physical performance.

**ENVIRONMENTAL HAZARDS:**
Exposure to extreme weather conditions, natural disasters, or hazardous terrain features such as cliffs, avalanches, or rockslides can result in injuries or accidents requiring emergency response and evacuation

# VARIOUS TYPES OF INJURIES THAT ONE MIGHT EXPERIENCE WHILE IN THE WILD:

## INSECT BITES AND STINGS:

Encountering insects such as mosquitoes, ticks, bees, or wasps can result in bites or stings, leading to itching, swelling, and allergic reactions.

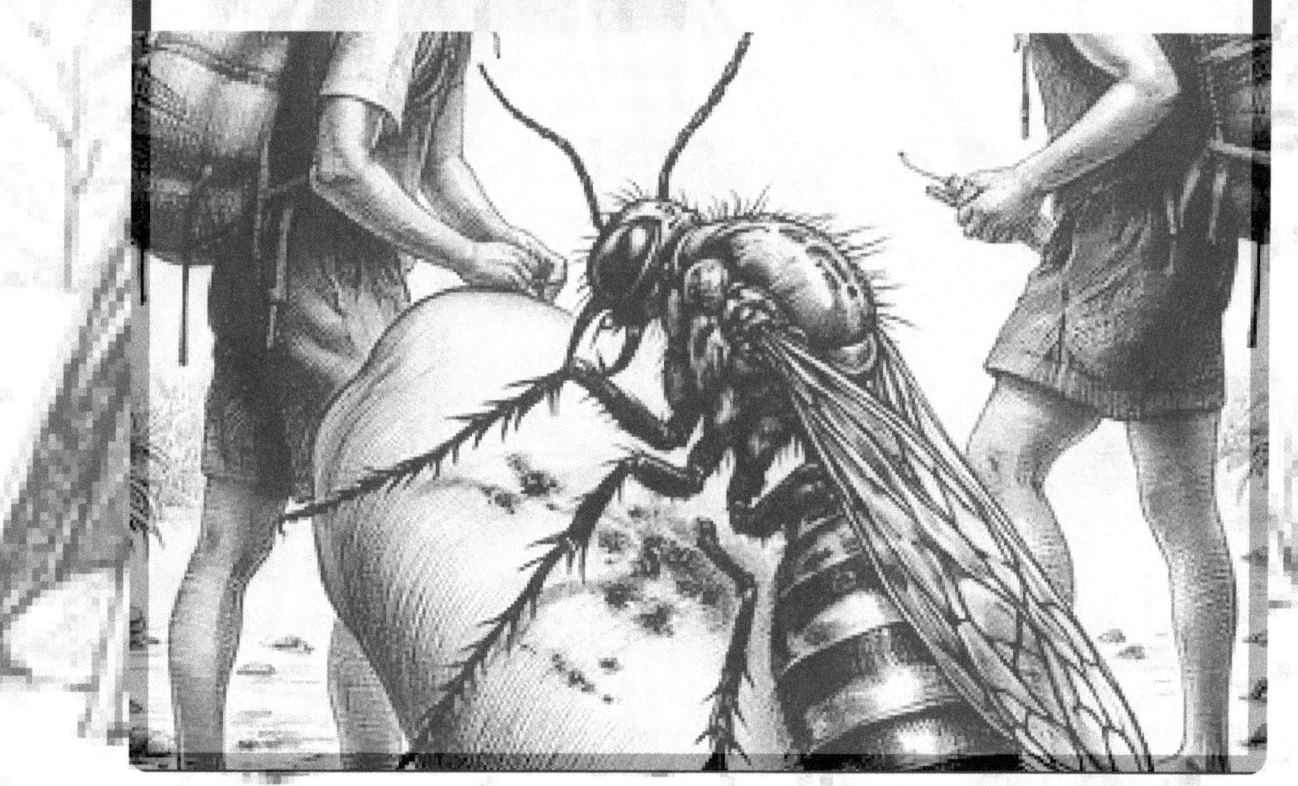

# BASIC FIRST AID GUIDELINES FOR ADDRESSING COMMON WILDERNESS INJURIES

These steps provide basic first aid guidelines for addressing common wilderness injuries, but it's important to seek professional medical help whenever possible, especially for severe or life-threatening conditions.

## SPRAINS AND STRAINS:

Rest the injured area.

Apply ice or cold pack to reduce swelling.

Compress the area with an elastic bandage.

Elevate the injured limb to reduce swelling.

51

# BASIC FIRST AID GUIDELINES FOR ADDRESSING COMMON WILDERNESS INJURIES

## FRACTURES:

Immobilize the injured limb with a splint.
Apply ice or cold pack to reduce swelling.
Seek medical attention immediately for
proper diagnosis and treatment.

# BASIC FIRST AID GUIDELINES FOR ADDRESSING COMMON WILDERNESS INJURIES

## CUTS AND LACERATIONS:
Clean the wound with soap and water.
Apply direct pressure to control bleeding.
Cover the wound with a sterile bandage or dressing.
Seek medical attention for deep or contaminated wounds

## INSECT BITES AND STINGS:
Remove the stinger if present (for bee stings).
Wash the area with soap and water.
Apply a cold compress to reduce pain and swelling.
Monitor for signs of allergic reaction and seek medical help if necessary.

# BASIC FIRST AID GUIDELINES FOR ADDRESSING COMMON WILDERNESS INJURIES

## BURNS:
Remove the heat source and cool the burn with cold water.
Cover the burn with a sterile dressing.
Do not pop blisters.
Seek medical attention for severe burns or large affected areas.

## HYPOTHERMIA:
Move to a warm shelter and remove wet clothing.
Wrap in blankets or use body heat to warm up.
Drink warm liquids if conscious.
Seek medical help immediately.

54

# BASIC FIRST AID GUIDELINES FOR ADDRESSING COMMON WILDERNESS INJURIES

## HEAT EXHAUSTION AND HEATSTROKE:
Move to a cooler environment and rest.
Drink cool fluids and remove excess clothing.
Apply cool compresses to the skin.
Seek medical help if symptoms worsen or if heatstroke is suspected.

## DEHYDRATION:
Drink small sips of water or oral rehydration solutions.
Rest in a shaded area and avoid exertion.
Cool the body with damp cloths or a cool bath.
Seek medical attention if symptoms persist or worsen.

# BASIC FIRST AID GUIDELINES FOR ADDRESSING COMMON WILDERNESS INJURIES

## ANIMAL ENCOUNTERS:

Slowly back away from the animal without making sudden movements.

Do not run or make direct eye contact.

Make yourself appear larger by raising your arms or opening your jacket.

If attacked, use any available objects as a barrier between you and the animal

## ALLERGIC REACTIONS:

Administer an epinephrine auto-injector if available.

Remove any stingers or foreign objects from the skin.

Monitor breathing and vital signs.

Seek immediate medical attention for severe reactions.

# HOW TO USE THE MAP AND COMPASS

By following these steps and using a map and compass effectively, you can navigate through the wilderness with confidence and find your way back to safety, even when lost or disoriented.

# HOW TO USE THE MAP AND COMPASS

**TO NAVIGATE WITH A MAP AND COMPASS IN THE WILDERNESS WHEN LOST:**

1. Orient the map to match the surrounding terrain and identify landmarks.
2. Determine your destination and draw a straight line to it on the map.
3. Take compass bearings by aligning the compass with your destination on the map.
4. Follow the compass bearing, adjusting your direction as needed.
5. Check your progress by comparing landmarks with the map.
6. Use identifiable features to confirm your position and adjust your route.
7. Reorient as necessary to stay on course until reaching your destination.

# HOW TO USE A SIGNALLING MIRROR FOR NAVIGATION AND ATTRACTING ATTENTION IN CASE OF EMERGENCY

Using a signaling mirror in the wilderness involves two main purposes: navigation and attracting attention.

Practice using the mirror beforehand and choose a clear, sunny day for optimal effectiveness.

# HOW TO USE A SIGNALLING MIRROR FOR NAVIGATION AND ATTRACTING ATTENTION IN CASE OF EMERGENCY

## FOR NAVIGATION:

1. Find a clear line of sight.

2. Hold the mirror correctly and aim the flash toward your target.

3. Flash the signal and repeat as necessary to guide your navigation.

# HOW TO USE A SIGNALLING MIRROR FOR NAVIGATION AND ATTRACTING ATTENTION IN CASE OF EMERGENCY

## FOR ATTRACTING ATTENTION:

1. Choose an open area with a clear view of potential rescuers.
2. Hold the mirror correctly and aim the flash toward the target.
3. Flash the signal in short bursts to attract attention, using SOS if needed.

# BUILDING A TENT

1. Gather materials
2. Select location
3. Set up support structure
4. Secure the tent
5. Stabilize the tent
6. Adjustment and finishing touches

# BUILDING A TENT

Building a detachable tent for wilderness survival can be a practical solution for shelter. Here's a step-by-step guide:

## 1.GATHER MATERIALS:

Tarp or waterproof material for the tent body.
Tent poles or sturdy branches for support.
Rope or cordage for securing the tent.
Stakes or heavy objects to anchor the tent to the ground.

# BUILDING A TENT

## 2.SELECT A LOCATION:

Choose a flat and elevated area away from potential hazards like flood zones, falling branches, or rocky terrain.

## 3.SET UP SUPPORT STRUCTURE:

Lay out the tarp or waterproof material on the ground where you want the tent to be.
Insert tent poles or position sturdy branches at each corner of the tarp to serve as support beams.

64

# BUILDING A TENT

## 4.SECURE THE TENT:

Use rope or cordage to tie one end of the tarp to each support pole or branch. Pull the tarp tight and secure the opposite ends to the remaining support poles or branches.

## 5.STABILIZE THE TENT:

Use stakes or heavy objects to anchor the corners of the tarp to the ground, ensuring stability in windy conditions.

# BUILDING A TENT

## 6. ADJUSTMENTS AND FINISHING TOUCHES:

Make any necessary adjustments to ensure the tent is taut and secure.
Fold over any excess material or reinforce seams with additional rope if needed.

## 7. DETACHABLE DESIGN:

To make the tent detachable, use clips or hooks to attach the tarp to the support structure instead of tying it directly.
This allows for easy removal and reattachment of the tarp, making it convenient to disassemble and transport the tent when necessary.

# BUILDING A TENT

## 8. TEST AND ADJUST:

Once the tent is assembled, test its stability and durability by gently pulling and pushing on the structure.
Make any final adjustments to ensure the tent is securely anchored and capable of withstanding outdoor elements.

## 9. MAINTENANCE AND CARE:

Regularly inspect the tent for any signs of wear or damage, and make repairs as needed to ensure its integrity.
Properly pack and store the tent when not in use to prolong its lifespan and effectiveness for future wilderness adventures.

# BUILDING A
# FIRE

# BUILDING A FIRE

A step-by-step guide on how to build a fire in the wilderness, with or without a lighter and in different weather conditions:

## 1.GATHER MATERIALS:

Collect tinder, such as dry leaves, grass, or bark, for igniting the fire.

Gather kindling, small sticks, and branches, ranging from pencil to finger thickness, to fuel the initial flames.

Collect larger fuelwood, such as logs or branches, to maintain the fire once it's lit.

# BUILDING A FIRE

## 2.PREPARE THE FIRE PIT:

Clear away any flammable materials from the area around the fire pit, creating a safe zone.

Build a ring of rocks or dig a shallow pit to contain the fire and prevent it from spreading.

## 3.PREPARE THE TINDER BUNDLE:

Create a tinder bundle by loosely arranging the dry tinder materials into a nest-like structure.

Ensure the tinder bundle is airy and fluffy to catch fire easily

# BUILDING A FIRE

**4.LIGHTING THE FIRE WITH A LIGHTER:**
Hold the lighter close to the tinder bundle
and ignite it with a steady flame.
Blow gently on the tinder bundle to
encourage the flames to spread.

**5.Building the Fire:**
Gradually add small kindling sticks to the
burning tinder bundle, arranging them in a
teepee or log cabin formation.
Once the kindling catches fire, add larger
fuelwood gradually to build up the flames.

# BUILDING A
# FIRE

## 6.MAINTAINING THE FIRE:

Feed the fire with additional fuelwood as needed to maintain a steady flame and heat. Monitor the fire and adjust the size and arrangement of the wood to control the intensity of the flames.

## 7.EXTINGUISHING THE FIRE:

Allow the fire to burn down to ash and embers before extinguishing it completely. Pour water over the fire and stir the ashes to ensure all embers are extinguished. Disperse the cooled ashes and ensure the fire pit is thoroughly extinguished.

# BUILDING A FIRE

## WITHOUT A LIGHTER OR A MATCHBOX:

**Using Alternative Fire Starters:**

Use natural fire-starting methods such as a flint and steel, fire starter rod, or magnifying glass to ignite the tinder bundle.

If available, use friction-based methods such as a bow drill or hand drill to create sparks and ignite the tinder.

# BUILDING A
# FIRE
## DIFFERENT WEATHER CONDITIONS:

## DRY WEATHER:

Exercise caution to prevent wildfires by ensuring the fire is contained within the fire pit and keeping the surrounding area clear of flammable materials. Be mindful of windy conditions that can spread embers and flames and take precautions to shield the fire from gusts.

## WET WEATHER:

Seek out dry tinder and kindling materials, such as dead standing wood or bark from fallen trees, to ensure the fire can ignite despite damp conditions. Use waterproof fire starters or create makeshift shelters to protect the fire from rain or moisture.

# FIRE SAFETY

**Safety precautions to follow while building a
fire in the wilderness to avoid outbreaks:**

1. Select a suitable location away from
overhanging branches, dry grass, or other
flammable materials.
2. Clear the area around the fire site, removing
any debris and creating a fire ring with rocks or
digging a pit.
3. Gather firewood, ensuring it is dry and
properly seasoned to minimize smoke and reduce
the risk of sparks.
4. Keep a bucket of water, a shovel, or a fire
extinguisher nearby for quick response to any
unexpected flare-ups.

# FIRE SAFETY

5. Start the fire using safe methods such as a lighter, matches, or a fire starter, avoiding accelerants like gasoline or lighter fluid.

6. Monitor the fire closely while it burns, ensuring it remains contained within the fire ring or pit.

7. Never leave the fire unattended and fully extinguish it before leaving the area or going to sleep.

8. Dispose of ashes properly by scattering them in the designated area or packing them out with you if necessary.

# SOURCING FOR WATER AND FOOD

Sourcing water and food in the wilderness is essential for survival. Here's how to do it:

# SOURCING FOR WATER AND FOOD

**WATER SOURCING:**

**1.NATURAL SOURCES:**
Look for streams, rivers, lakes, or ponds where water is likely to collect.
Collect rainwater using containers or by improvising catchment systems with tarps or large leaves.

**2.PLANTS:**
Learn to identify water-bearing plants such as cacti, bamboo, or vines, and extract water from them.
Look for dew on plants in the early morning and collect it using absorbent materials like clothing or bandanas.

# SOURCING FOR WATER AND FOOD

### 3.DIGGING WELLS:

If near a sandy area, dig a hole a few feet deep and wait for water to seep into it.
Filter the collected water through cloth or natural materials to remove debris and impurities.

### WATER PURIFICATION:

Boil water over a fire to kill bacteria and parasites.
Use water purification tablets or drops to chemically treat water and make it safe for drinking.
Construct a simple filtration system using sand, charcoal, and cloth to remove impurities from water.

# SOURCING FOR WATER AND FOOD

**FOOD SOURCING:**

## 1.FORAGING:

Learn to identify edible plants, berries, nuts, and mushrooms in the wilderness.
Look for wild fruits, berries, and nuts growing on trees or bushes.
Avoid plants with thorns, shiny leaves, or a bitter taste, as they may be poisonous.

## 2.HUNTING AND TRAPPING:

Set up traps using natural materials such as sticks, rocks, and vines to catch small game like rabbits, squirrels, or birds.
Use improvised weapons like spears or slingshots to hunt larger game if available.
Fish in streams, rivers, or lakes using handmade fishing gear such as hooks, lines, and bait made from natural materials.

# SOURCING FOR WATER AND FOOD

## 3.INSECTS AND SMALL CREATURES:

Look for insects, grubs, or worms under rocks, logs, or leaf litter, and consume them for protein.

Catch small reptiles, amphibians, or insects for food, ensuring they are safe to eat and properly cooked.

## 4.FISHING:

Craft simple fishing gear using improvised hooks, lines, and bait made from natural materials.

Fish in calm, shallow waters using nets, traps, or improvised fishing rods.

Use bait such as insects, worms, or small fish to attract larger fish.

# SOURCING FOR WATER AND FOOD

**PRESERVATION:**
Smoke, dry, or jerk meat to preserve it for longer-term storage.
Utilize natural preservation methods such as pickling or fermenting to extend the shelf life of foraged or hunted foods.

By mastering these skills and techniques, individuals can effectively source water and food in the wilderness, increasing their chances of survival in challenging environments.

# SEEKING FOR HELP IN THE WILDERNESS

Seeking help in the wilderness during an emergency is crucial for ensuring safety and survival. Here's how to do it:

## 1.STAY CALM:

Maintain a calm and composed demeanour to think clearly and make rational decisions.

## 2.ASSESS THE SITUATION:

Evaluate the severity of the emergency and determine the immediate threats to safety. Check for injuries among yourself and others in your group and administer first aid as needed.

# SEEKING FOR HELP IN THE WILDERNESS

## 3.SIGNAL FOR HELP:

Use signalling devices such as whistles, signal mirrors, or flare guns to attract attention from rescuers.

Create visible signals on the ground or in open areas using rocks, branches, or brightly colored clothing to indicate your location.

## 4.MAKE NOISE:

Yell, shout, or blow a whistle at regular intervals to alert nearby individuals or search parties to your presence.

Use a loud noise-making device such as an air horn or whistle to increase your chances of being heard over long distances.

# SEEKING FOR HELP IN THE WILDERNESS

## 5.UTILIZE COMMUNICATION DEVICES:

Use a cell phone, satellite phone, or two-way radio to call for help if you have reception or access to emergency services.

Send distress signals via text message, email, or satellite communication devices if voice communication is unavailable.

## 6.USE NAVIGATION TOOLS:

Consult maps, compasses, or GPS devices to determine your exact location and provide accurate coordinates to rescuers.

Leave markings or signs along trails or at landmarks to guide search teams to your location.

# SEEKING FOR HELP IN THE WILDERNESS

## 7.STAY PUT:

If you're lost or injured, stay in one place to avoid further confusion or risk of injury.
Set up a visible campsite with shelter, water, and food supplies to wait for rescuers to arrive.

## 8.CREATE SMOKE SIGNALS:

Build a small, controlled fire during daylight hours to create smoke signals visible from the air or a distance.
Use green vegetation or damp materials to produce thick, white smoke that contrasts against the surrounding environment.

# SEEKING FOR HELP IN THE WILDERNESS

## 9.SIGNAL AIRCRAFT:

Wave brightly colored clothing or objects to catch the attention of passing aircraft.
Lay down in an open area and create large "X" or "SOS" symbols using rocks, branches, or other materials to signal overhead aircraft.

## 10.FOLLOW SEARCH AND RESCUE PROCEDURES:

Listen for search aircraft or ground teams and respond to their signals or calls for attention.
Cooperate with rescue personnel and follow their instructions to facilitate your safe extraction from the wilderness.

# CONCLUSION

Reflecting on the adventures and experiences gained during your time in the wilderness, it's clear that this journey has been nothing short of transformative. From the rugged terrain to the serene beauty of nature, each moment spent exploring the great outdoors has left an indelible mark on your soul.

As you prepare to return home, carry with you the memories of breathtaking sunsets, invigorating hikes, and moments of quiet solitude amidst the wilderness. Let these experiences serve as a reminder of the resilience and strength within you, and may they inspire future adventures yet to come.

# CONCLUSION

Though your time in the wilderness may be ending, the lessons learned and the connections forged will remain etched in your heart forever. As you journey homeward, may you carry the spirit of the wilderness with you, finding solace and inspiration in the memories of your wild and untamed adventures.